DATE DUE

PRINTED IN U.S.A.

AWASH IN COLOUR

Great American Watercolours from the
Museum of Fine Arts, Boston

NATIONAL GALLERY OF SCOTLAND
EDINBURGH

First published 1996
by the Trustees of the National Galleries of Scotland
for the exhibition *Awash in Colour: Great American Watercolours from the Museum of Fine Arts, Boston*
at the National Gallery of Scotland, Edinburgh, 26 April – 14 July 1996
and *The Great American Watercolour* at the Rijksmuseum,
Amsterdam, 10 August – 27 September 1996
© all rights reserved

ISBN 0 903598 60 4

Designed and typeset in Linotype Fairfield by Dalrymple
Printed on 150gsm Consort Royal Satin, manufactured by UK Paper, Donside
Printed and bound by BAS Printers Ltd
Over Wallop

Front cover: Winslow Homer *The Blue Boat* (detail) 1892
Back cover: Edward Hopper *Anderson's House* 1926
Frontispiece: John Singer Sargent *Simplon Pass: The Lesson* (detail) 1911
Illustrated on page 16: Maurice Prendergast
Handkerchief Point (detail) 1896–7

Preface

Awash in Colour is a remarkable exhibition of over fifty watercolours, selected from the magnificent holdings of the Museum of Fine Arts in Boston, being shown in Europe for the first time at the National Gallery of Scotland, Edinburgh and the Rijksmuseum, Amsterdam. The Museum of Fine Arts holds an unparalleled collection of nearly two thousand American watercolours, many of which have rarely been shown, even in America.

Few of the names and reputations of even the finest nineteenth- and early twentieth-century American watercolourists have reached a wide European audience. Extraordinarily, this is the first major exhibition of American watercolours to be shown in Europe. The remarkable watercolours of two artists in particular will stand out in this selection: John Singer Sargent, who from an early age travelled widely in Europe, and Winslow Homer, the most influential of all the nineteenth-century American watercolourists, who spent two years crucial to his career working on the Northumberland coast in the fishing village of Cullercoats.

The National Gallery of Scotland and the Rijksmuseum are most grateful to Malcolm Rogers, the Ann and Graham Gund Director of the Museum of Fine Arts, Boston and to his predecessor, Alan Shestack for making possible this truly exceptional loan. Thanks should also go to the following colleagues at the Museum of Fine Arts for their contributions to the success of this exhibition; Brent R. Benjamin; Katherine G. Getchell; Theodore E. Stebbins, Jr; Clifford S. Ackley; Roy L. Perkinson; Annette Manick; Gail M. English; Carl F. Zahn; Cynthia M. Purvis; Gilian Wohlauer; Patricia

Loiko and Kim H. Pashko. Above all, special thanks are due to Sue Welsh Reed and Carol Troyen for their work on the text of this catalogue.

The exhibition consists of a selection of works from a larger show held at the Museum of Fine Arts in Boston in 1993. It has been organised in exchange for an exhibition the Rijksmuseum is preparing of *Dutch Drawings and Prints from around 1900* which will be held in Boston in the near future. The directors of the Rijksmuseum would like to thank all their colleagues who have collaborated in the preparation of this exhibition.

Among the many staff of the National Galleries of Scotland whose skills and efforts have contributed to the success of both the catalogue and the exhibition, particular thanks are due to Janis Adams and Margaret Mackay, and above all to Mungo Campbell who initially suggested and has overseen the project in Edinburgh.

An exhibition such as this is a major undertaking. The final word of thanks must go to the sponsors of the exhibition. In Scotland, we are grateful to The British Linen Bank, celebrating its two hundred and fiftieth anniversary in 1996. The Bank is an award winner under the Pairing Scheme (the National Heritage Arts Sponsorship Scheme) for its support of *Awash in Colour*. The Pairing Scheme is a Government scheme managed by the Association for Business Sponsorship for the Arts. The sponsor in Amsterdam is Deloitte & Touche, Accountants, Tax Lawyers and Management Consultants. Deloitte & Touche, while dedicated to the art of business, is also an enthusiastic supporter of art and culture in the Netherlands and in particular the Rijksmuseum.

TIMOTHY CLIFFORD
Director, National Galleries of Scotland

MICHAEL CLARKE
Keeper, National Gallery of Scotland

HENK VAN OS
General Director, Rijksmuseum

PETER SCHATBORN
Keeper, Rijksprentenkabinet

Introduction

THE first works of art produced in America by Europeans were watercolours – views of the Atlantic coast and its native inhabitants, painted by the artist-explorers Jacques Le Moyne and John White in the late sixteenth century. For three hundred years, military men, scientists, and adventurers continued to use this portable and adaptable medium for the purpose of documenting the New World. British naval officers sketched topographical views of harbours, John James Audubon and other naturalists recorded flora and fauna, and explorers engaged such artists as Thomas Moran to capture the splendours of the Far West [no. 32]. As the country became more settled and cities grew, watercolour was put to more peaceful and domestic purposes. The brothers Archibald and Alexander Robertson emigrated from Aberdeen to New York City, where they founded the Columbian Academy in the 1790s, and taught a generation of water-colourists to paint picturesque landscapes based on the writings of the English amateur painter and theorist, the Rev. William Gilpin. In the eighteenth century, American schoolgirls were taught to embroider but, by about 1820, they painted their memorials and fancy subjects in watercolours. In some of these, the brushstrokes still resemble stitches taken with needle and silken thread.

Advances in technology made watercolour increasingly attractive and accessible to an ever growing number of practitioners. In 1780, William Reeves, a London pigment manufacturer or 'colour man', began to mix dry powdered pigments with a binder and press them into hard little cakes that were easily portable in a box. In the 1840s, these dry cakes were superseded by moist, more intense, colours packaged in pans and collapsible metal tubes, which required less effort to dissolve in water. In addition, new synthetic colours cost less and increased the range of hues possible without mixing.

Growing interest in watercolour led American artists to form specialised professional organisations designed to feature the medium and elevate its status. After several short-lived starts, the American Watercolor Society – modelled on Britain's Society of Painters in Watercolours (1804) – was founded in New York in 1866; it is still active. Watercolour associations were founded in other American cities as well, for example, the Boston Watercolor Society (for men only), organised in 1885, was followed in 1887 by the Boston Watercolor Club (initially for women but later open to men). The annual exhibitions of these organisations encouraged collectors and the public to appreciate watercolours as distinct and significant works of art.

In New York in the 1860s and 1870s watercolour exhibitions were dominated by a group of Americans who emulated the English Pre-Raphaelite painters. This style was promoted by the English artist, critic and writer, John Ruskin, whose books and ideas influenced a number of American artists. Like their British counterparts, these Americans used brilliant colours and thick, opaque pigments in their watercolours, which were often large and ambitious and looked much like oil paintings. Henry Roderick Newman's *Mount Everett from Monument Mountain in April* [no. 33] demonstrates the almost scientific fidelity to nature that Ruskin advocated, whereas William Trost Richards's *Near Paradise, Newport, Rhode Island* [no. 37] has the presence of an oil painting. The expression of nature's forces that Ruskin so admired in the work of the English master J. M. W. Turner is vividly evoked in the American scenes of James Hamilton and Thomas Moran [nos. 6 and 32].

In Boston, watercolour was widely practised by both men and women who learned from private tutors. In 1896, a local writer commented on the city's 'army of water-colourists'; these practitioners and an equally enthusiastic group of Boston patrons helped to shape and develop the collection of the Museum of Fine Arts, Boston. They purchased watercolours by La Farge, Homer and other Americans, and had a particular taste for works by Anton Mauve, Jacob Maris and other Dutch artists of the Hague School.

Although many oil painters, such as George Inness [no. 25], made watercolours on their travels to distant lands, watercolour was not part of the professional art school curriculum in America, except as it was used for architectural rendering and design. In the 1870s, John La Farge used watercolours to plan the mural decorations and stained glass windows of Boston's Trinity Church. By the late seventies he was painting elegant watercolours of flowers for exhibition and sale. The delicacy of *Wild Roses in an Antique Chinese Bowl* [no. 26], with its pale colours and fragile, translucent blossoms, makes a striking contrast to the bold and vivid work of La Farge's friend, Winslow Homer. Both artists found a ready market for their watercolours, profiting from the growing tendency in America to admire the medium and take it seriously.

Among the greatest treasures in the Museum of Fine Arts's exceptional collection of American art are its extensive holdings of watercolours by Winslow Homer and John Singer Sargent, generally acknowledged as America's greatest masters of the medium. Lloyd Goodrich, a leading Winslow Homer scholar, observed in 1945: 'Bostonians have always been great collectors of watercolors, for some occult reason, perhaps connected with thrift: and in buying [Homer's] watercolors they also showed that other character-istic Boston trait, discrimination.' In 1899 the Museum of Fine Arts purchased the first watercolour by Homer to enter an American museum. There are now forty-five Homer watercolours in the Museum's collection, beginning with his sunny images of children outdoors, painted during summer holidays in the 1870s. During Homer's extended stay at Cullercoats, on the north east coast of England, in the early 1880s, his technique became much more sophisticated as he mastered the traditional English watercolour style. Laying out his compositions with broad, overlapping washes of colour, he created a range of colouristic and textural effects by both adding pigment and subtracting it by rewetting and blotting, and by scraping. Homer was one of the first American artists to exploit the texture and colour of the paper itself by leaving areas white and unpainted.

In the 1890s, Homer painted in the wilderness of New York State's Adirondacks region and in the Caribbean, working in daring and innovative ways as he explored the capacity of watercolour to be both descriptive and expressive. *The Blue Boat* [no. 17] and *The Sponge Diver* [no. 19] demonstrate the unequalled mastery with which he used pure, transparent pigments, especially when depicting water. The pristine condition of *The Blue Boat* provides a rare opportunity to appreciate the original glowing luminosity of Homer's colours. In the last quarter of the nineteenth century, Winslow Homer not only changed the face of watercolour painting but also revolutionised the status of the medium in America. As early as 1879, a review of his work stated: 'Mr Winslow Homer goes as far as anyone has ever done in demonstrating the value of watercolors as a serious means of expressing dignified artistic impressions.' The success of Homer's watercolours inspired subsequent generations of artists to work in the medium; he was hailed as 'America's master in watercolor' against whose direct, natural style and technical mastery the achievements of all others were measured.

For John Singer Sargent, watercolour was a holiday medium, one he turned to for relief from the formal and social demands of portrait painting. Sargent worked in watercolour while vacationing in the Italian Alps, in Tuscany and on the sun-drenched Greek island of Corfu. His subjects are generally informal – corners of gardens, Alpine meadows, family members and friends casually posed and sometimes dressed in exotic costumes – and such unlikely themes as laundry hanging on a line [no. 42]. Sargent called watercolour 'making the best of an emergency'. He termed his subjects 'snapshots', as though to underscore the medium's inherent spontaneity and to suggest that his pictures were painted directly and effortlessly. In fact, Sargent's watercolours were carefully thought out and rendered with a host of complex techniques and a lively mixture of transparent and opaque pigments, sometimes applied straight from the tube. The resulting compositions, filled with tinted shadows, dappled light and dazzling streaks of intense colour, are among Sargent's most beautiful and imaginative works.

Sargent never intended his watercolours for exhibition or sale. However, in 1909 he agreed to show his work of the previous season at Knoedler's gallery in New York. Almost the entire group – some eighty-three watercolours – was bought by the Brooklyn Museum in New York. As a further testimony to Sargent's popularity, three years later, the Museum of Fine Arts, Boston, purchased forty-five watercolours made in Italy between 1908 and 1911; several other major museums followed suit. These works were heralded in the press and were exhibited in large shows (often displayed with water-colours by Winslow Homer) that gave new prestige to the medium. Sargent's water-colours influenced a whole generation of painters who enthusiastically embraced his casual subject matter and bravura style.

Sargent's interest in light and his technical sophistication were shared by many of his contemporaries. The freely painted, light-filled and brilliantly coloured images of Childe Hassam and Ross Turner, among others, take full advantage of watercolour's fluidity and spontaneity; these artists developed the impressionist style in a medium that their French counterparts seldom explored. Although Maurice Prendergast shared the Impressionists' enthusiasm for images of middle-class, outdoor, recreation and leisure, his style was even more adventurous than theirs. Prendergast characteristically used a high horizon line to focus attention on the surface of his sheet and dotted his images with anonymous figures, individualised only by posture and dress. Areas of bright white paper and a scattering of eye-catching opaque reds give his watercolours the almost abstract, patterned quality of a mosaic [no. 35].

The interest in abstraction and the devotion to watercolour as an experimental medium linked Prendergast with many of the most creative artists of the early twentieth century. In the teens, John Marin, Charles Demuth and, for a time, Georgia O'Keeffe chose watercolour as their primary medium, finding its luminosity ideal for rendering the fragmented, transparent surfaces of the cubist vision. In the 1920s, such artists as Charles Burchfield and Edward Hopper found watercolour's ability to suggest texture especially advantageous as they explored a realist style. In the hands of these artists, watercolour contributed significantly to the advancement of progressive art in America.

Marin, Demuth and O'Keeffe were bolstered in their efforts by the photographer and dealer, Alfred Stieglitz, who consistently promoted their work in solo shows at his famous art gallery at 291 Fifth Avenue in New York. Stieglitz showed Marin's watercolours there almost annually from 1909 and O'Keeffe's, to great acclaim, in 1917 and again in 1923.

From the early years of the twentieth century, Stieglitz had sought out the most advanced art of the day. Works on paper were especially welcome; wash drawings by Rodin made their American debut here in 1908, as did Cézanne's watercolours in 1911. These shows had a dramatic effect on young American painters and provided support for their own stylistic experiments – experiments encouraged by the versatility and spontaneity of watercolour. Defying conventional notions of finish, the American avant-garde expanded watercolour's techniques and materials. Marin used charcoal and opaque pigments as well as traditional transparent washes; he reportedly worked with both hands, applying paint with brushes, matchsticks, his fingers and even syringes [no. 31]. Demuth sometimes painted on cheap, thin, writing paper; in later works, he left large expanses of paper bare and created patterned textural effects through careful blotting and lifting of pigment [no. 5]. In a series of remarkable watercolours painted between 1916 and 1918, O'Keeffe skillfully manipulated washes so that, as colours bled into one another, they defined contours and produced subtle tonal variations [no. 34].

By the early 1920s, American achievements in watercolour caused the progressive critic Henry McBride to crow, 'we are beating the world in watercolors, just now'. His boast reflects the pre-eminence of the American watercolour school, and the fact that watercolour, once dismissed as 'lighter fare', had come to be taken seriously by both private collectors and museums. Entries to the annual exhibitions of the American Watercolor Society, which showcased the work of established, traditional painters, increased markedly in the period after World War 1. And in 1921, the Brooklyn Museum mounted the landmark *Group Exhibition of WaterColor Paintings by American Artists*. Hailed as 'the best collection of American watercolors that has ever been seen ... a service to art, artists, and the country', the exhibition was prefaced with a gallery dedicated to Homer, Sargent, La Farge and Prendergast. It then focused on the moderns, especially Marin, Demuth and William and Marguerite Zorach. By beginning with the turn-of-the-century masters, the exhibition identified the younger watercolourists as heirs to a great legacy. The show also boosted such newcomers as Charles Burchfield, who worked extensively in watercolour, and Edward Hopper, who would become famous as an oil painter but who painted his breakthrough works in watercolour.

Burchfield painted watercolours on the scale of oils, and expanded the capabilities of the medium by working against its natural properties [no. 1]. 'I virtually abandoned the pointed brush [preferred by most watercolourists] for the sable *bright* brush, which allowed a more robust, firm stroke, similar indeed to the oil on canvas technique'. He made underdrawings with granular charcoal rather than with the usual delicate graphite and worked on large sheets, often with opaque paints, using his brush to create texture. His surreal, dream-like nature studies, often monumental in scale, address a quintessentially American theme, which he termed 'the big epic power of nature'.

Hopper's first major New York exhibition, held at the Frank Rehn Gallery in 1924, consisted of sixteen watercolours that introduced many of the themes – drab Victorian houses, lighthouses silhouetted against the sky, faded urban landscapes – that he would later popularise in oil paintings. Hopper's technique was as controlled as Burchfield's was expansive: he avoided exotic papers, rare pigments, accidental effects and flashy techniques, favouring instead thin, transparent washes carefully laid down in small, measured strokes. His deliberately inelegant, yet luminous, surfaces are perfectly suited to his stark, undecorative subject matter [no. 22]. According to Burchfield, Hopper's 'modest, unobtrusive – almost impersonal – way of putting on paint' yielded pictures 'provocative in their terseness'.

The accessibility and democratic nature of watercolour may explain why so many American artists, from Homer and Sargent to Marin and Burchfield, were attracted to the medium. Its materials were inexpensive and easily portable. It was not taught at the country's principal art academies. And – with the exception of the British school – European artists, whose contributions in painting and sculpture many Americans found daunting, had rarely chosen it for major artistic statements. Unhampered by such traditions, many enterprising American artists made their mark in watercolour. Although often small in scale, these watercolours are monumental in feeling. Their dazzling colour and technical variety demonstrate the fresh, creative vision of American watercolourists, who have made one of the United States's most original contributions to the history of art.

SUE W. REED AND CAROL TROYEN

NOTE: *In the plate section, the watercolours are arranged chronologically, except in the case of multiple works by one artist which have been kept together. The catalogue, at the end of the book, is arranged alphabetically by artist. In given dimensions, height precedes width.*

Colour Plates

SUNSET ON THE JERSEY FLATS, 1861

Mount Everett from Monument Mountain in April, 1867

Cliffs, Green River, Wyoming, 1872

THE GREEN RIVER, WYOMING, 1871

BEACH WITH SUN DRAWING WATER, 1872

NEAR PARADISE, NEWPORT, RHODE ISLAND, 1877

CASTLE IN THE MOUNTAINS, c. 1873

WILD ROSES IN AN ANTIQUE CHINESE BOWL, 1880

MOONLIT SEASCAPE, c.1883

VIEW OVER KYOTO FROM YA AMI, 1886

LOOKING DOWN OVER RICE-FIELDS
1891

BO-PEEP (GIRL WITH SHEPHERD'S CROOK SEATED BY A TREE), 1878

BOY AND GIRL ON A HILLSIDE, 1878

DRIVING COWS TO PASTURE, 1879

Children Playing under a Gloucester Wharf, 1880

GIRLS ON A CLIFF, 1881

Girl with Red Stockings (The Wreck), 1882

Street Corner, Santiago de Cuba, 1885

ADIRONDACK LAKE, 1889

TROUT BREAKING (RISE TO THE FLY), 1889

THE BLUE BOAT, 1892

40   Old Settlers, 1892

THE SPONGE DIVER, 1898–9

42

Nocturne, Railway Crossing,
Chicago, 1893   43

A GARDEN IS A SEA OF FLOWERS, 1912

GENOA: THE UNIVERSITY
c.1908

CORFU: LIGHTS AND SHADOWS, 1909

UNDER THE RIALTO BRIDGE, *c.*1909

THE GARDEN WALL, 1910

LA BIANCHERIA, 1910

VILLA DI MARLIA: LUCCA, 1910

SIMPLON PASS: THE FOREGROUND, 1911

SIMPLON PASS: THE TEASE, 1911

SIMPLON PASS: THE LESSON, 1911

CARRARA: WORKMEN, 1911

JOHN SINGER SARGENT

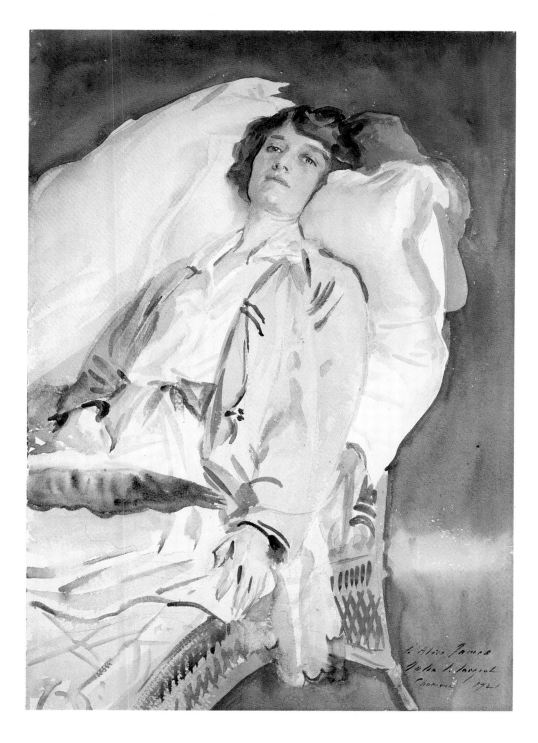

ALICE RUNNELLS JAMES
(MRS WILLIAM JAMES), 1921   57

HANDKERCHIEF POINT, 1896–7

Clouds and Mountains at Kufstein, 1910

CROTCH ISLAND, MAINE, THE COVE, 1924

GEORGIA O'KEEFFE

RED AND BLACK, 1916

61

EGG PLANTS AND PEARS, 1925

SHEEP ISLAND, MAINE, 1919

66   WINTER BOUQUET, 1933

DECK OF A BEAM TRAWLER, 1923

ANDERSON'S HOUSE, 1926

HOUSE OF THE FOG HORN, NO. 2, 1927

FIRST BRANCH OF THE WHITE RIVER, VERMONT, 1938

MR RIVER'S GARDEN, 1942

Catalogue

CHARLES BURCHFIELD

born 1893, Ashtabula Harbour, Ohio–died 1967, West Seneca, New York

Burchfield studied at the Cleveland School of Art and worked for a time as an accountant before moving to Buffalo, in upstate New York, in 1921. After several years working in the design department of a wallpaper company, Burchfield devoted himself to painting full time in 1929, prior to a one-man exhibition at the Museum of Modern Art in New York in 1930. Most of Burchfield's prolific output of both urban and natural landscapes is in watercolour, a medium which he often handled with bold presence, using broad, flat brushes and opaque paints applied much in the manner of oil painting.

1 WINTER BOUQUET, 1933
Illustrated on page 66
Transparent and opaque watercolour over graphite and charcoal on moderately thick, cream wove paper, affixed overall to thick grey cardboard, 910 × 688mm
Signed and dated lower right in black wash: monogram CEB / 1933
Ellen K. Gardner Fund. 34.43

2 IN MAY, 1939
Illustrated on page 67
Watercolour with touches of black crayon on thick, cream wove paper, 632 × 504mm
Signed and dated lower right in black crayon: monogram CEB/1939
Hayden Collection, Charles Henry Hayden Fund. 39.762

SAMUEL COLMAN

born 1832, Portland, Maine – died 1920, New York City

Colman grew up in New York, where his father was a successful publisher and print dealer. He began to exhibit landscapes at the National Academy of Design in his late teens, often painting the scenery of the Hudson River and the White Mountains. After studying in France, Spain and Morocco in the early 1860s, Colman helped to found the American Watercolor Society in 1866. In 1870, using the newly established railway network which was opening up the country, Colman made the first of several painting expeditions into the West. By the late 1870s he was one of the most highly prized watercolour painters in America. Colman's finished exhibition watercolours reflect his belief that the medium could rival the presence of oil painting.

3 THE GREEN RIVER, WYOMING, 1871
Illustrated on page 22
Transparent and opaque watercolour over graphite, with pen and brown ink on thick, moderately rough, cream wove paper, 410 × 554mm
Signed and dated lower left in brown ink: Saml Colman. 1871
M. & M. Karolik Collection. 53.2442

CHARLES DEMUTH

born 1883 – died 1935, Lancaster, Pennsylvania

Demuth trained as a painter at the Pennsylvania Academy of the Fine Arts. Most of his career was divided between his native provincial Pennsylvania and the cosmopolitan bohemian circles of Paris and New York. From 1912–14 he studied in Paris where he attended the academies Julian, Moderne and Colarossi. His response to developments in modern European painting was most particularly reflected in the numerous sensuous figurative watercolours painted after his return to America. While Demuth's watercolours of the early 1920s reflected the abstractionist developments to be found in Cubism, his depictions of the forms and textures in the American urban landscape were very much his own. Weakened by diabetes during the 1920s, he continued to paint until his death, producing a notable series of still lifes in watercolour.

4　IN THE PROVINCE (ROOFS), 1920
Illustrated on page 62
Opaque watercolour over graphite on very thick cardboard ('Beaver Board', a multilayered building material), 602 × 504mm
Signed and dated lower left in graphite: C. Demuth 1920 / Lancaster Pa.
Inscribed verso, left centre in graphite: Roofs / In the Province # 1 / C. Demuth / Lancaster Pa / 1920-
Anonymous gift in memory of Nathaniel Saltonstall. 68.790

5　EGG PLANTS AND PEARS, 1925
Illustrated on page 63
Opaque and transparent watercolour over graphite on moderately thick, slightly textured, off-white wove paper; partial watermark: 1924 UNBLEACHED ARNOLD, 354 × 507mm
Signed and dated centre left in graphite: C. Demuth-/ 1925-
Inscribed centre right in graphite: Lancaster PA.
Bequest of John T. Spaulding. 48.765

JAMES HAMILTON

born 1819, near Belfast, Ireland – died 1878, San Francisco, California

Hamilton spent most of his life in Philadelphia, where his family had emigrated when he was fifteen. He had some formal training as a draughtsman before exhibiting his first canvas in 1840. Popular for his maritime subjects, Hamilton was given the soubriquet, the 'American Turner', the influence of the British artist being particularly apparent in his work after an extended visit to England in 1854–5. In 1875 he sold more than one hundred paintings at auction to finance a trip round the world. He only got as far as San Franscico, where he died in 1878.

6　SUNSET ON THE JERSEY FLATS, 1861
Illustrated on page 19
Transparent and opaque watercolour on moderately thick, light grey wove paper, mounted on cardboard, 226 × 424mm
Signed and dated lower left in brown wash: J. Hamilton / 1861
M. & M. Karolik Collection. 61.283

CHILDE HASSAM

born 1859, Dorchester, Massachusetts – died 1935, East Hampton, Long Island

Hassam started his career as an illustrator and engraver for the Boston publisher, Little, Brown & Co. From his first one-man exhibition in Boston in 1882, watercolours formed a major and successful part of Hassam's output. The artist studied in Paris for three years from 1886, during which time his painting was heavily influenced by Impressionism. Hassam settled in New York on his return to America. During the 1890s, Hassam developed his technique beyond the transparent washes and light palette which typify his European and New England watercolours, showing a masterful ability to manipulate the medium to great effect.

7　NOCTURNE, RAILWAY CROSSING, CHICAGO, 1893
Illustrated on page 43
Opaque watercolour on thick, rough-textured cream wove paper, 406 × 298mm. Signed lower left in black watercolour: Childe Hassam. Inscribed verso in black ink: Nocturne / Railway Crossing Chicago / Childe Hassam
Hayden Collection. Charles Henry Hayden Fund. 62.986

❧ WINSLOW HOMER

born 1836, Boston, Massachusetts – died 1910, Prout's Neck, Maine

Homer had almost no formal training as a painter. After serving an apprenticeship as a lithographer, he worked for many years as a freelance illustrator, in Boston and then in New York, where he became particularly well known for the work that appeared in *Harper's Weekly* both during and after the Civil War. Homer also pursued a career in painting, first exhibiting in 1863 at the National Academy of Design. After spending several months in Paris in 1867, he returned to America where he settled in New York once more. During the 1870s, Homer began to use watercolour extensively during summer visits to New England. Homer spent most of 1881–2 in Britain, working mainly at Cullercoats, near Tynemouth on the Northumbrian coast. On his return to America he settled in Maine, where he built a studio by the ocean and worked on his great marine canvases. He travelled for sports fishing and to paint his popular watercolours: to the Adirondacks in summer, and in winter to the Caribbean. Homer developed a monumental and poetic approach to the medium which marks him out as one of the finest of all watercolour painters of the nineteenth century.

8 BO-PEEP (GIRL WITH SHEPHERD'S CROOK SEATED BY A TREE), 1878
Illustrated on page 30
Opaque watercolour over graphite on medium, smooth, tan wove paper mounted on cardboard, 178 × 210mm
Signed and dated at lower right in pen and black ink: Homer / 78
On verso of cardboard in graphite various inscriptions and sketches
Bequest of John T. Spaulding. 48.724

9 BOY AND GIRL ON A HILLSIDE, 1878
Illustrated on page 31
Watercolour over graphite on thick, rough-textured, cream wove paper, 225 × 288mm
Signed and dated lower right in black wash: HOMER 1878
Bequest of the Estate of Katherine Dexter McCormick. 68.568

10 DRIVING COWS TO PASTURE, 1879
Illustrated on page 32
Watercolour over graphite on thick, slightly textured, cream wove paper, 217 × 345mm
Signed and dated lower left in black wash: HOMER '79
Bequest of the Estate of Katherine Dexter McCormick. 68.569

11 CHILDREN PLAYING UNDER A GLOUCESTER WHARF, 1880
Illustrated on page 33
Watercolour over graphite on thick, rough-textured, cream wove paper, 205 × 342mm
Signed and dated lower right in black wash: HOMER 1880
On verso in graphite (in Homer's hand): 41. (outlined); No 19 [?] – A / 13¾ × 8½ / mat to come close to / edge not cove at all
Hayden Collection. Charles Henry Hayden Fund. 21.2554

12 GIRLS ON A CLIFF, 1881
Illustrated on page 34
Opaque and transparent watercolour over graphite on very thick, rough-textured, cream wove paper, 322 × 485mm
Signed and dated lower left in grey wash: Winslow Homer / 1881
On verso in pen and brown ink (probably Homer's hand):
19 (crossed out)
Bequest of David P. Kimball in memory of his wife Clara Bertram Kimball. 23.522

13 GIRL WITH RED STOCKINGS (THE WRECK), 1882
Illustrated on page 35
Watercolour over graphite on very thick, slightly textured, cream wove paper, 342 × 495mm
Signed and dated lower right in brown wash: HOMER / 1882
On verso in graphite (in Homer's hand): Girl with Red Stockings; 48. (outlined)
Bequest of John T. Spaulding. 48.727

14 STREET CORNER, SANTIAGO DE CUBA, 1885
Illustrated on page 36
Watercolour over graphite on thick, rough textured, cream wove paper, 356 × 509mm
Signed and titled at lower right in black watercolour: Homer / Santiago de / Cuba
Anonymous gift in memory of Horace D. Chapin. 1978.300

15 ADIRONDACK LAKE, 1889
Illustrated on page 37
Watercolour over graphite on moderately thick, slightly textured, cream wove paper, 355 × 508mm
Signed and dated lower right in black wash: HOMER 1889
On verso in graphite: M E Homer
William Wilkins Warren Fund. 23.215

16 TROUT BREAKING (RISE TO THE FLY), 1889
Illustrated on page 38
Watercolour over graphite on moderately thick, slightly textured, cream wove paper, 353 x 506mm
Signed and dated at lower left in graphite: Homer 1889; also signed at lower left (above graphite signature) in red watercolour: Homer 89
On verso at lower right in brown watercolour: Homer / 1889
Bequest of John T. Spaulding. 48.729

17 THE BLUE BOAT, 1892
Illustrated on page 39
Watercolour over graphite on very thick, slightly textured, off-white wove paper, 386 × 546mm
Signed, dated and inscribed lower left in pen and brown ink: Winslow Homer N.A. 1892 / This will do the business
On verso in pen and brown ink (Homer's hand): K 15 × 21; in graphite (possibly Homer's hand): On the Trail
Bigelow Collection. Bequest of William Sturgis Bigelow. 26.764

18 OLD SETTLERS, 1892
Illustrated on page 40
Watercolour over graphite on very thick, moderately textured, dark cream wove paper, 547 × 386mm
Inscribed on verso in pen and brown ink (Homer's hand): P – 15 × 21
Bequest of Nathaniel T. Kidder. 38.1412

19 THE SPONGE DIVER, 1898–9
Illustrated on page 41
Watercolour over graphite on moderately thick, moderately rough, cream wove paper; partial Whatman watermark: MAN 1898, 380 × 543mm
Inscribed in brush and black wash: H. and Bahamas 1889 (lower left); Homer / 1889 (lower right) On verso in graphite (in Homer's hand): No 18
Gift of Mrs Robert B. Osgood. 39.621

20 PALM TREES, FLORIDA, 1904
Illustrated on page 42
Watercolour over graphite on moderately thick, slightly textured, cream wove paper, 502 × 352mm
Inscribed lower right in graphite: Sketch W. H.
Bequest of John T. Spaulding. 48.731

EDWARD HOPPER

born 1882, Nyack, New York – died 1967, New York City

Hopper's initial training was as a commercial artist, before transferring to the New York School of Art in 1900. Although he visited Europe several times over the next few years, Hopper absorbed little of contemporary European painting and, on settling in New York, earned his living as an illustrator while developing his career as a printmaker and painter. After many years without critical or financial success, Hopper finally developed the mature style on which his fame rests through his watercolours of urban American architecture, produced during the early 1920s. He was to remain a prolific watercolourist for some twenty years, using the medium with a matter-of-fact robustness which helped to instil his frequently unremarkable subject matter with an often remarkably powerful presence.

21 DECK OF A BEAM TRAWLER, 1923
Illustrated on page 68
Watercolour over graphite on moderately thick, slightly textured, cream wove paper, 298 × 457mm. Signed and dated lower left in grey wash: Edward Hopper / Gloucester 1923
Bequest of John T. Spaulding. 48.715

22 ANDERSON'S HOUSE, 1926
Illustrated on page 69
Watercolour over graphite on moderately thick, slightly textured, cream wove paper, 354 × 508mm
Signed lower left in black wash: Edward Hopper / Gloucester
Bequest of John T. Spaulding. 48.720

23 HOUSE OF THE FOG HORN, No. 2, 1927
Illustrated on page 70
Watercolour over graphite on moderately thick, slightly textured, cream wove paper, 352 × 506mm
Signed lower right in blue ink: Edward Hopper / Two Lights, Me
Bequest of John T. Spaulding. 48.722

24 FIRST BRANCH OF THE WHITE RIVER, VERMONT, 1938
Illustrated on page 71
Watercolour over graphite on very thick, rough-textured, cream wove paper; watermark: HAND MADE J. WHATMAN 1936 ENGLAND, 553 × 683mm
Signed lower right in blue-green watercolour: EDWARD HOPPER
William Emerson Fund. 39.43

GEORGE INNESS

born 1824, Newburgh, New York – died 1894, Bridge of Allan, Scotland

Inness is best known for canvases which owe much to the Barbizon painters whom he encountered on several visits to France during the 1850s. In 1870, after a decade producing such pictures for a receptive market, Inness returned to Europe, living in Italy for four years where he produced many of his most successful oil paintings and his most original watercolours. In spite of his prodigious output in oils, fewer than fifty watercolours by the artist are known.

25 CASTLE IN THE MOUNTAINS, c.1873
Illustrated on page 25
Transparent and opaque watercolour over graphite on moderately thick, light tan wove paper, 224 × 308mm, irregular
Signed lower left in graphite: Geo. Inness
Inscribed on verso in graphite: G Inness
M. & M. Karolik Collection. 60.1026

JOHN LA FARGE

born 1835, New York City – died 1910, Providence, Rhode Island

The son of prosperous French émigré parents, La Farge received drawing and watercolour lessons as a child, although he did not finally settle on a career as a professional painter until 1859, after a visit to Paris where he studied briefly in the studio of Thomas Couture. His first landscapes and flower paintings of the early 1860s found little success and it was only during the 1870s that his decorative designs for murals, stained glass and applied art objects were fully recognised with the first in a series of major commissions. La Farge made a number of journeys to the Far East and the South Pacific, including a year-long voyage round the world in 1890–1. In his later years, La Farge published extensively on the theory, criticism, and appreciation of art, and on his travels. One of his closest artistic friends was Winslow Homer.

26 WILD ROSES IN AN ANTIQUE CHINESE BOWL, 1880
Illustrated on page 26
Transparent and opaque watercolour on thick, slightly textured, cream wove paper, 276 × 229mm
Initialed and dated lower right in black wash: JLF / 1880
Bequest of Miss Elizabeth Howard Bartol. Res. 27.96

27 MOONLIT SEASCAPE, *c.*1883
Illustrated on page 27
Transparent and opaque watercolour on moderately thick, smooth, cream wove paper, 170 × 123mm
Bequest of Miss Mary C. Wheelwright. 59.688

28 VIEW OVER KYOTO FROM YA AMI, 1886
Illustrated on page 28
Transparent and opaque watercolour over graphite on thick, slightly textured, cream wove paper, 268 × 369mm
Inscribed in pen and black ink: Sept 17.86 (lower left); LF / Kioto / 86 (lower right); other notes in graphite
Gift of William Sturgis Bigelow. 21.1441

29 VIEW IN CEYLON, NEAR DAMBULLA, LOOKING DOWN OVER RICE-FIELDS, 1891
Illustrated on page 29
Transparent and opaque watercolour on moderately thick, smooth, dark cream wove paper, 430 × 342mm. Inscribed lower right: LF.91. (in black wash); near Dambulla Ceylon (in graphite)
Gift of William Sturgis Bigelow. 26.784

JOHN MARIN

born 1870, Rutherford, New Jersey – died 1953, Cape Split, Maine

John Marin is one of several twentieth-century American painters known principally as a watercolourist, and for whom stylistic developments in watercolour paved the way for advances in other media. His reputation rests on his prolific output of watercolour landscapes, urban and rural, produced both out of doors and in his studio. After training at the Pennsylvania Academy of the Fine Arts and then in New York, Marin spent five years in Europe between 1905–10. During the early part of his career, his etchings and drawings took their inspiration particularly from those of Whistler. After his return from Europe, however, Marin's painting increasingly expressed the powerful forces which he found in nature as abstract and decorative but nonetheless recognisable images. Many of these dramatic watercolours were painted in Maine, where he spent most of his summers after 1920. One of Marin's greatest champions was the photographer, Alfred Stieglitz, who, with his wife Georgia O'Keeffe, amassed a major collection of the artist's work.

30 CLOUDS AND MOUNTAINS AT KUFSTEIN, 1910
Illustrated on page 59
Watercolour on moderately thick, rough-textured, off-white wove paper, 393 × 472mm
Signed and dated lower left in blue watercolour: Marin 10
Hayden Collection. Charles Henry Hayden Fund. 61.1139

31 CROTCH ISLAND, MAINE, THE COVE, 1924
Illustrated on page 60
Watercolour, black crayon and a pointed tool (brush handle?) on thick, rough-textured, white wove paper, partially affixed to cardboard to which silver leaf has been applied, 366 × 451mm
Signed and dated lower right in blue watercolour and black crayon: Marin '24
Signed and dated on verso in graphite: Crotch Island Maine / 1924. / The Cove
Signed on reverse of original silver mat in graphite: Crotch Island Maine / The Cove – 1924
Hayden Collection. Charles Henry Hayden Fund. 61.1140

THOMAS MORAN

born 1837, Bolton, Lancashire – died 1926, Santa Barbara, California

Moran's reputation rests chiefly on his powerful evocations of the unique landscapes of the West, particularly the Rocky Mountains. Thomas Moran's father, a weaver, emigrated with his family to Philadelphia in 1844. After serving an apprenticeship as a wood engraver, Moran was encouraged to pursue painting by James Hamilton, whose work is also included in this exhibition. During the 1860s, Moran made several visits to Europe. He spent 1861–2 in England studying J. M. W. Turner's oils and watercolours in London, and drawing sites in the British Isles. In 1866–7 he and his wife were in France and Italy where he came to know Corot. In 1871 Moran's career took a significant turn when he was commissioned to serve as staff artist on an expedition to explore the Yellowstone region. This experience laid the foundations for Moran's favourite subject matter, the mountains and waters of the Rockies, and he returned there many times over the next two decades before settling in California in 1916. Like J. M. W. Turner, whose work he much admired, Moran used the smallest watercolours to extraordinary effect to conjure dramatic landscapes of enormous scale.

32 CLIFFS, GREEN RIVER, WYOMING, 1872
Illustrated on page 21
Watercolour over graphite on thick, smooth, beige wove paper, 158 × 297mm
Signed lower right in brush and brown wash: (monogram) TMoran. / 1872
M. & M. Karolik Collection. 60.428

HENRY RODERICK NEWMAN

born 1843, Easton, New York – died 1917, Florence, Italy

Newman grew up in New York, where he took up painting in 1861, after abandoning his studies at medical school. After teaching at the Cooper Institute in New York from 1865–6, he moved to Massachusetts where he painted a number of watercolours which were influenced by Pre-Raphaelite painting in their highly keyed and brilliant use of colour and their close observation and 'truth to nature'. Newman moved to Europe in 1870, and finally settled in Florence where he painted its architectural monuments as well as the flowers of the Tuscan countryside. His work, almost entirely in watercolour, was much admired by John Ruskin, whom he met on a visit to England in 1879. Newman also painted in Venice, in Egypt in the 1880s and 1890s, and in Japan between 1896 and 1898.

33 MOUNT EVERETT FROM MONUMENT MOUNTAIN IN APRIL, 1867
Illustrated on page 20
Watercolour over graphite on thick, smooth, dark cream wove paper, 266 × 351mm
Signed and dated lower centre in red wash: H. R. NEWMAN / 67
Gift of Mrs Harriet Ropes Cabot. 50.2630

GEORGIA O'KEEFFE

born 1887, Sun Prairie, Wisconsin – died 1986, Santa Fe, New Mexico

After studying at the Art Institute of Chicago and then in New York, O'Keeffe worked for a time as a commercial artist before moving to Texas where she supervised art teaching in public schools. She returned to New York to study at Columbia University in 1914. In 1915 O'Keeffe began a series of extraordinary abstract drawings which were shown to her future husband Alfred Stieglitz, who exhibited them without her permission. O'Keeffe returned to Texas in 1916, where for two years she worked as an art teacher while developing her landscape painting. From 1918–28 she lived in New York. In 1929, O'Keeffe made her first lengthy visit to New Mexico, where she settled after Stieglitz's death in 1949, and where she found the landscapes which inspired her most famous images.

34 RED AND BLACK, 1916
Illustrated on page 61
Watercolour on moderately thick, slightly textured, tan wove paper,
300 × 225mm
M. & M. Karolik Fund and The Hayden Collection. 1993.90

MAURICE PRENDERGAST

born 1858, St John's, Newfoundland – died 1924, New York City

Prendergast was one of the most sophisticated painters of his generation. Although his formal training was limited to study at the Académie Julian and at Colarossi's studio in Paris, he was well acquainted with the art literature of his day, particularly that detailing modern movements. Prendergast's family had moved to Boston in 1868 where he continued to live with his brother, his lifelong companion, until 1914, when he moved to New York. By the 1880s the brothers' aptitude for art had attracted the attention of local patrons who encouraged them to travel abroad. Maurice went to England in 1886–7 and France in 1891–4. In 1898–9, sponsored by a prominent Boston collector, he toured Italy, painting many watercolours that are still considered his most glorious works. Underlying Prendergast's attractive and accessible subject matter was a use of colour and a tendency to abstraction which marked him out as one of the most avant-garde American painters at the turn of the century.

35 HANDKERCHIEF POINT, 1896–7
Illustrated on pages 16 & 58
Watercolour over graphite on thick, moderately rough-textured,
cream wove paper, 505 × 350mm
Signed lower right in graphite: Prendergast – / Pre
*Gift of Francis W. Fabyan in memory of Edith Westcott Fabyan.
31.906*

✒ WILLIAM TROST RICHARDS

born 1833, Philadelphia, Pennsylvania – died 1905, Newport, Rhode Island

Although Richards had little formal training as a painter, through his early employment as a metalwork designer he developed considerable ability as a draughtsman. After an extensive journey to Europe in 1855–6, Richards started to work full time as a landscape painter. After another visit to Europe during the mid-1860s he became particularly interested in marine and coastal subjects, working extensively for the first time in watercolour. These closely observed and highly atmospheric works brought Richards considerable success during the 1870s.

36 BEACH WITH SUN DRAWING WATER, 1872
Illustrated on page 23
Opaque watercolour over graphite on moderately thick, slightly textured, light beige wove paper, 172 × 353mm
Signed lower left in brown ink: Wm. T. Richards. 1872
M. & M. Karolik Collection. 60.1058

37 NEAR PARADISE, NEWPORT, RHODE ISLAND, 1877
Illustrated on page 24
Opaque watercolour over graphite on very thick, rough-textured, pink-buff wove paper ('carpet paper'), stretched and tacked on a wooden panel, 584 × 940mm
Signed and dated on lower left in black wash: Wm T. Richards. 1877; and on reverse of panel: Near Paradise, Newport / Wm T. Richards
Gift of Mrs Arthur Astor Carey. Res. 27.154

✒ JOHN SINGER SARGENT

born 1856, Florence, Italy – died 1925, London, England

Sargent's father had been a doctor in Philadelphia before abandoning his practice to travel with his wife in Europe. Sargent's first exposure to art came from his mother, who was a capable watercolourist; as a consequence, he was encouraged to sketch as a child. As a teenager, he produced a remarkable series of sketchbooks filled with accomplished watercolour records of his family's constant travels. In the 1880s and 1890s he made watercolours on various trips to Spain, North Africa and Venice, as well as on holiday in the Cotswolds; these were often in preparation for other projects. It was only in the early 1900s that he began to regard his watercolours as independent compositions and to exhibit these and then to sell them. Major groups of watercolours were exhibited and sold in New York beginning in 1909. Because the watercolours were the product of his holidays and travels, they were often highly personal in composition, as brilliant in their dazzling facility as his formal society portraits, though often highly experimental in technique.

38 GENOA: THE UNIVERSITY, c.1908
Illustrated on page 45
Watercolour over graphite, with wax resist on thick, rough-textured, cream wove paper; watermark: J.WHATMAN, 530 × 405mm
Signed lower left in iron gall ink: John S. Sargent
Hayden Collection. Charles Henry Hayden Fund. 12.204

39 CORFU: LIGHTS AND SHADOWS, 1909
Illustrated on page 46
Transparent and opaque watercolour over graphite on thick, rough-textured, cream wove paper, 403 × 530mm
Hayden Collection. Charles Henry Hayden Fund. 12.207

40 UNDER THE RIALTO BRIDGE, c.1909
Illustrated on page 47
Transparent and opaque watercolour over graphite on moderately thick, moderately rough-textured, cream wove paper, 276 × 484mm
Hayden Collection. Charles Henry Hayden Fund. 12.203

41 THE GARDEN WALL, 1910
Illustrated on page 48
Transparent and opaque watercolour over graphite, with wax resist, on thick, rough-textured, cream wove paper; with fragmentary (Whatman?) watermark, 381× 459mm
Signed upper left in red watercolour: John S. Sargent; upper right in iron gall ink: John S. Sargent
Hayden Collection. Charles Henry Hayden Fund. 12.222

42 LA BIANCHERIA, 1910
Illustrated on page 49
Transparent and opaque watercolour over graphite, with wax resist on thick, rough-textured, cream wove paper; fragmentary watermark: WHATMAN 1905 [?] ENGLAND,
403 × 530mm
Signed lower left in iron gall ink: John S. Sargent
Hayden Collection. Charles Henry Hayden Fund. 12.229

43 VILLA DI MARLIA: LUCCA, 1910
Illustrated on page 50
Watercolour over graphite, with wax resist, on thick, rough-textured, cream wove paper; fragmentary WHATMAN watermark, 404 × 533mm
Signed lower left in iron gall ink: John S. Sargent
Hayden Collection. Charles Henry Hayden Fund. 12.232

44 SIMPLON PASS: THE FOREGROUND, 1911
Illustrated on page 51
Transparent and opaque watercolour over graphite, with wax resist, on thick, rough-textured, cream wove paper; fragmentary WHATMAN watermark, 357 × 509mm
Signed lower right in iron gall ink: John S. Sargent
Hayden Collection. Charles Henry Hayden Fund. 12.219

45 SIMPLON PASS: THE TEASE, 1911
Illustrated on page 52
Transparent and opaque watercolour over graphite, with wax resist, on thick, rough-textured, cream wove paper, 401× 524mm
Signed lower right in iron gall ink: John S. Sargent
Hayden Collection. Charles Henry Hayden Fund. 12.216

46 SIMPLON PASS: THE LESSON, 1911
Illustrated on page 53
Transparent and opaque watercolour over graphite, with wax resist, on thick, rough- textured, cream wove paper, 381 × 459mm
Signed upper right in iron gall ink: John S. Sargent
Hayden Collection. Charles Henry Hayden Fund. 12.218

47 LIZZATORI I, 1911
Illustrated on page 54
Watercolour over graphite with wax resist on thick, rough-textured, cream wove paper; fragmentary WHATMAN watermark, 530 × 400mm
Signed lower left in graphite: John S. Sargent
Hayden Collection. Charles Henry Hayden Fund. 12.239

48 CARRARA: WORKMEN, 1911
Illustrated on page 55
Transparent and opaque watercolour over graphite with wax resist, on thick rough-textured, cream wove paper, 355 × 507mm
Signed lower right in iron gall ink: John S. Sargent
Hayden Collection. Charles Henry Hayden Fund. 12.235

49 THE CASHMERE SHAWL, 1911
Illustrated on page 56
Watercolour over graphite, with wax resist, on thick, rough-textured, cream wove paper, 507 × 355mm
Inscribed on verso, at centre right, in graphite: To be cut / as marked / on other side.
Hayden Collection. Charles Henry Hayden Fund. 12.227

50 ALICE RUNNELLS JAMES (MRS WILLIAM JAMES), 1921
Illustrated on page 57
Transparent and opaque watercolour over graphite on thick, rough-textured, cream wove paper, 534 × 342mm
Inscribed lower right in iron gall ink: to Alice James / John S. Sargent / Chocorua 1921
Gift of William James. 1977.834

ROSS TURNER

born 1847, Westport, New York – died 1915, Nassau, Bahamas

Turner was almost thirty before he began his career as a painter. After studying in Munich and visiting France and Italy, he settled in Boston in 1883. He found his greatest success as a watercolourist and most of his best work is in this medium. Turner became a noted teacher of watercolour, numbering among his pupils the poet Celia Thaxter, through whom he befriended Childe Hassam. The two painters spent many summers as Thaxter's guests on the Isles of Shoals, New Hampshire. Whereas Turner had earlier inspired Hassam to develop his interest in watercolour, by the mid-80s Hassam's vibrant style affected Turner's. Turner was an avid traveller and his watercolours record views in Italy, Mexico and Bermuda.

51 A GARDEN IS A SEA OF FLOWERS, 1912
Illustrated on page 44
Transparent and opaque watercolour on slightly textured, dark cream, commercially prepared illustration board, 527 × 780mm
Inscribed lower right in pale blue watercolour: a garden is a sea of flowers / Ross Turner / 1912
Gift of the Estate of Nellie P. Carter. 35.1690

ANDREW WYETH

born 1917, Chadds Ford, Pennsylvania

The watercolours of Wyeth are possibly some of the best known and most frequently reproduced of any living American artist in his native country. As a child, Wyeth was encouraged to draw by his father, a well-known illustrator, and he held his first one-man exhibition in New York at the age of twenty, in 1937. Initially, Wyeth worked in a very painterly manner, particularly recalling the work of Winslow Homer in numerous atmospheric images of the Maine coastline. During the late 1940s however, his technique became more precise. Wyeth's subject-matter, the people and landscapes of Maine and Pennsylvania, depicted with close and sometimes disquieting overtones, has remained much the same throughout his career.

52 MR RIVER'S GARDEN, 1942
Illustrated on page 72
Watercolour over graphite on moderately thick, rough, white wove paper; watermark: cᴬm WATERCOLOUR PAPER ENGLAND 1940, 450 × 752mm
Signed lower right in pen and black ink: Andrew Wyeth
Hayden Collection. Charles Henry Hayden Fund. 43.1

MARGUERITE ZORACH

born 1887, Santa Rosa, California – died 1968, Brooklyn, New York City

Marguerite Thompson grew up in California. She travelled extensively in Europe from 1908 before returning home via the Far East in 1912. In Paris, she studied for a time with the Scottish painter, John Duncan Fergusson. On her return to America, she eventually settled in New York and married the sculptor and painter, William Zorach. From 1916, she increasingly worked on textile and tapestry designs, and often collaborated closely with her husband. Zorach continued to paint and draw throughout her life, her watercolours reflecting, in their stylised and decorative appearance, her involvement in the applied arts.

53 SHEEP ISLAND, MAINE, 1919
Illustrated on page 64
Watercolour over graphite on moderately thick, slightly textured, off-white wove paper; watermark: ARNOLD FIBRE, 317 × 400mm
Signed lower right in black wash: M. ZORACH
Curator's Discretionary Fund. 1980.13

WILLIAM ZORACH

born 1889, Euberick, Lithuania – died 1966, Bath, Maine

William Zorach grew up in Cleveland. He studied there and in New York before going to Paris in 1910. While studying at the informal art school, La Palette, with the Scottish painter, John Duncan Fergusson, he met his future wife, Marguerite Thompson. After settling in New York, Zorach began to turn away from painting and, by the early 1920s, had established a reputation as a sculptor. Watercolour, however, remained an important medium throughout his life, especially in the recording of the natural landscape.

54 YOSEMITE FALLS, 1920
Illustrated on page 65
Watercolour over graphite on moderately thick, white wove paper, 472 × 346mm. Signed lower right in brown ink: – William Zorach –
Inscribed lower left in brown ink: Yosemite Falls 1920
Gift of Claire W. and Richard P. Morse. 1992.64